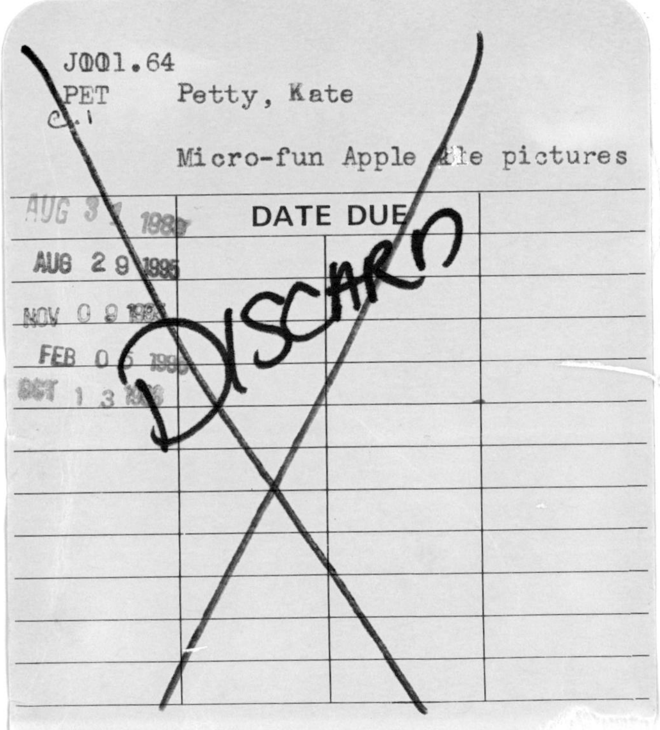

J 001.64
PET   Petty, Kate
c.1
Micro-fun Apple lle pictures
AUG 3   1980
AUG 2 9 1995
NOV 0 9 199
FEB 0 6 199
OCT 1 3 199
DATE DUE
DISCARD

PICTURES

AN ALADDIN BOOK

Design by Cooper-West, 70 Old Compton Street, London W1

Illustrations by Cooper-West and Tessa Barwick

Programs by Robin Betts, Adam Buckley, Marcus Milton, Les Rowley

Text by Kate Petty

First published in Great Britain in 1985 by
Franklin Watts, 12a Golden Square, London W1

First published in the United States in 1986 by
Gloucester Press, 387 Park Avenue South, New York NY10016

© Aladdin Books Ltd 1985

Designed and produced by
Aladdin Books Ltd, 70 Old Compton Street, London W1

ISBN 0-531-17018-7

Library of Congress
Catalog Card Number: 85-81979

Printed in Belgium

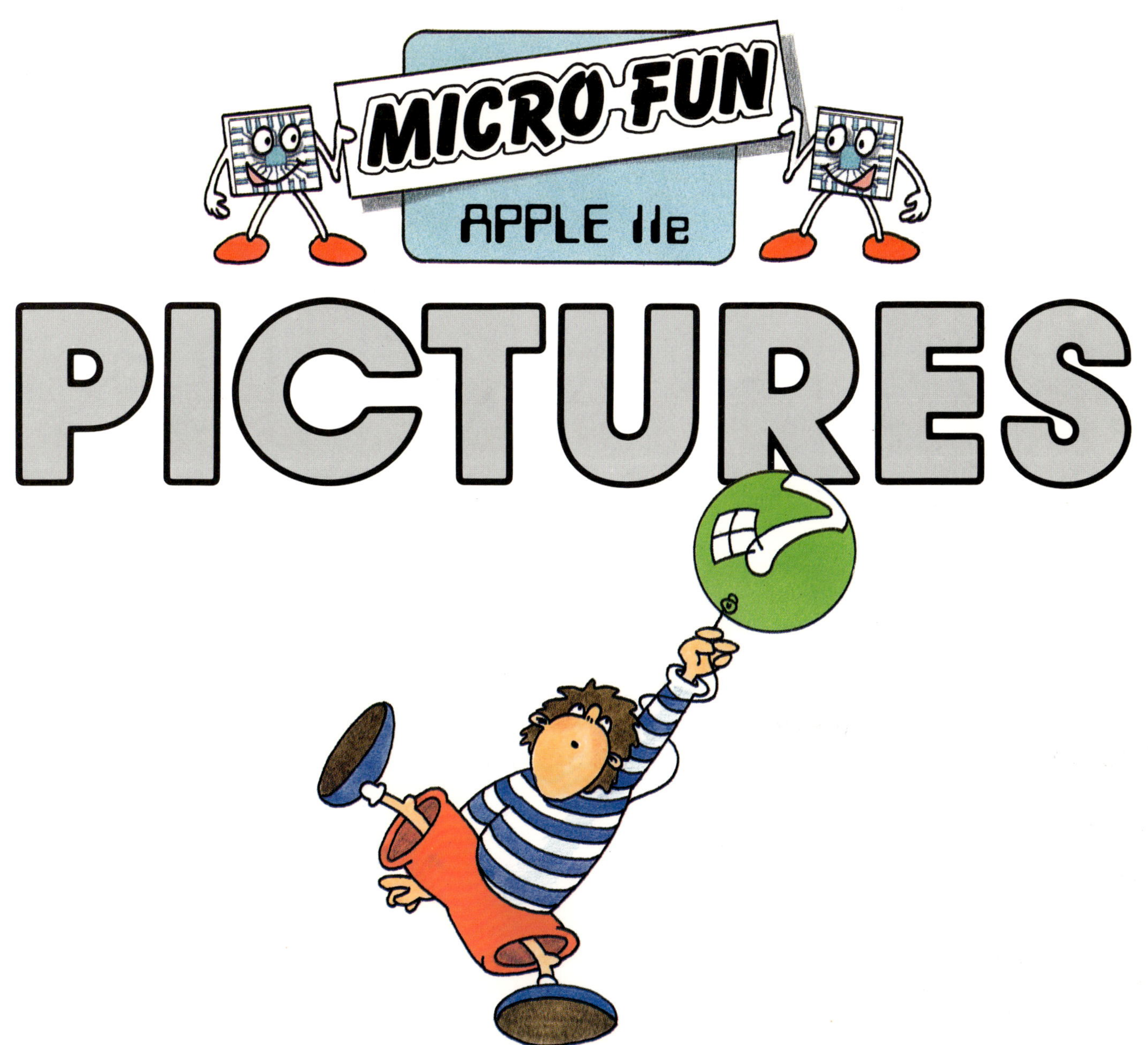

PICTURES

Gloucester Press
New York · Toronto · 1986

INTRODUCTION

This book will give you a lot of fun while you are getting to know your computer. The programs are simple to start with but they get longer and more complicated as you go on. Each program is complete in itself. The program is printed out for you to copy. Find out about the games and how to play them from the text. You can see how each one will look in the screen picture next to the program. You might want to add extra effects to some of the games. These can be found at the end of the book.

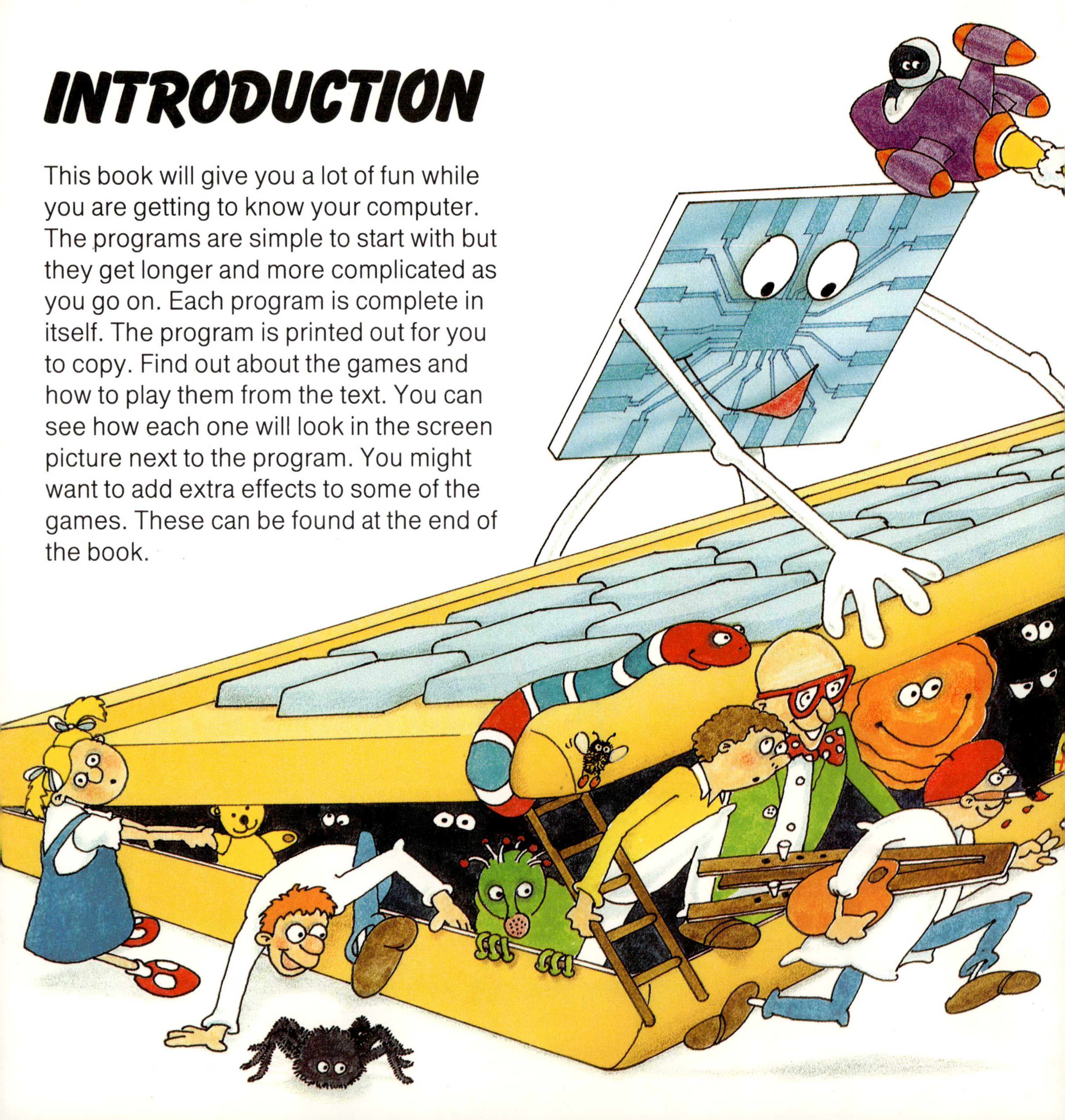

CONTENTS

YOUR COMPUTER

Get to know your keyboard. Some keys have two symbols. To print the top symbol you must hold down the **SHIFT** key before pressing the key you need. The programs in this book are printed in capital letters so press down the **CAPS LOCK** key before you start typing them in. Where you see this symbol ■ you must press the **space bar** once for each time it appears.

To load your tape
Rewind tape to starting point.
Type **LOAD "NAME"** and press **RETURN**.
Press PLAY on the tape recorder.
At the signal type **RUN** and press **RETURN** and you are ready to play.

Storing programs on tape
Type in the program.
Connect a tape recorder to the computer.
Insert a blank cassette.
Type **SAVE "NAME"** (for **"NAME"** type the first 10 letters of the name of the program inside quotes) and press **RETURN**.
Press PLAY and RECORD together on the tape recorder and press **RETURN** on the computer.
You will hear a tone.
Press STOP on the tape recorder when the noise ends.

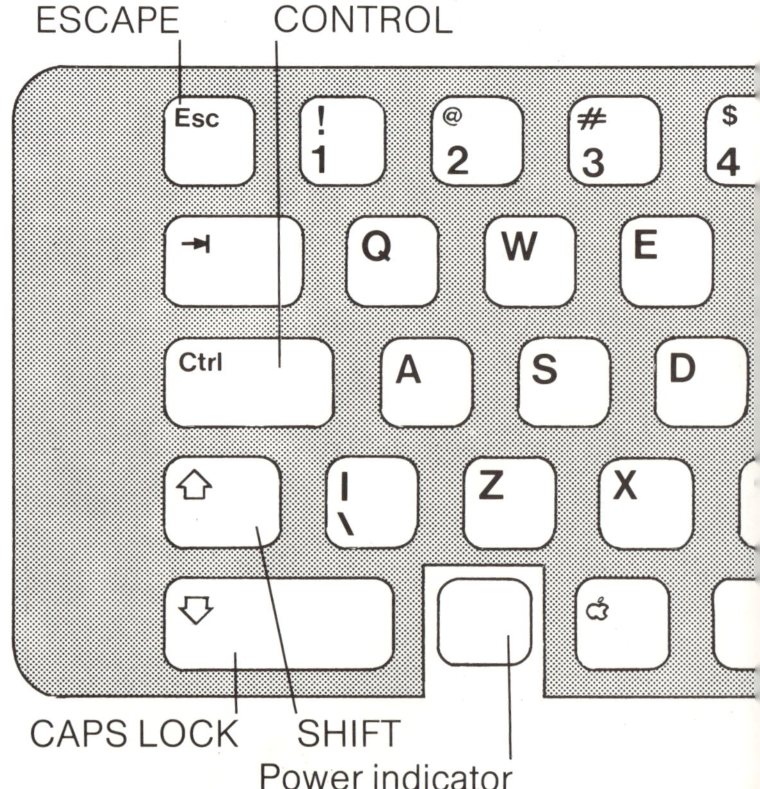

How to correct mistakes
To see the old program as you typed it press
CONTROL and RESET together, type HOME and
press RETURN. Then type LIST and press
RETURN. When you have found your mistake, press
ESCAPE and then use the up and left cursor keys
to get to the start of the line which contains the
mistake. Press the space bar once, and type the
correction over the old line. You can use the right
cursor key to skip over the parts of the old line
which are alright. Use the right cursor key to go to
the end of the corrected lines, and press RETURN.
Type LIST and press RETURN to see the program.

Multiply
Double quotes
Minus
RETURN
Plus
DELETE
RESET
Space bar
Divide
Cursor keys or arrow keys
SHIFT

EASY PICTURES

You can make all sorts of weird and wonderful images appear on your computer screen. You don't even need a program. Start by drawing this little face. Enter the three lines very carefully and press **RETURN** after each one. Your face will appear on the right-hand side of the screen.

HTAB 30:   PRINT "@■■■@"
HTAB 32:   PRINT "^"
HTAB 31:   PRINT "---"

Your screen has an invisible grid. Each line of the grid has a number. By typing in the number of the line you want any character to appear on, you can position your pictures on the screen. Try altering the numbers in the "face" instructions to move your face across the screen. You can make up new pictures by using the different characters on your keyboard.

HTAB 30 tells the computer to print whatever is between the quotes at column 30. If you change the numbers after **HTAB**, the parts of the face will move from side to side.

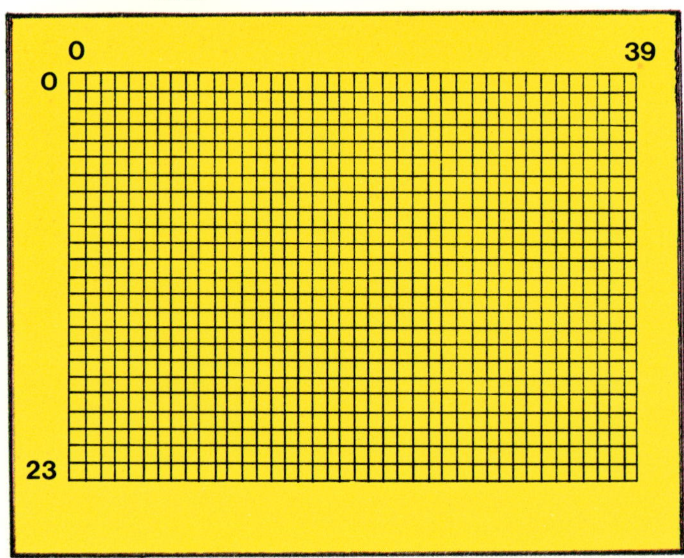

Now try this short program. Always press **RETURN** at the end of each line. Take particular care with the quotes and commas in line 60. When you have entered the program, type **RUN** and press **RETURN**. Then press any key to launch your rocket. Type **RUN** and press **RETURN** to relaunch. To add sound effects see page 28.

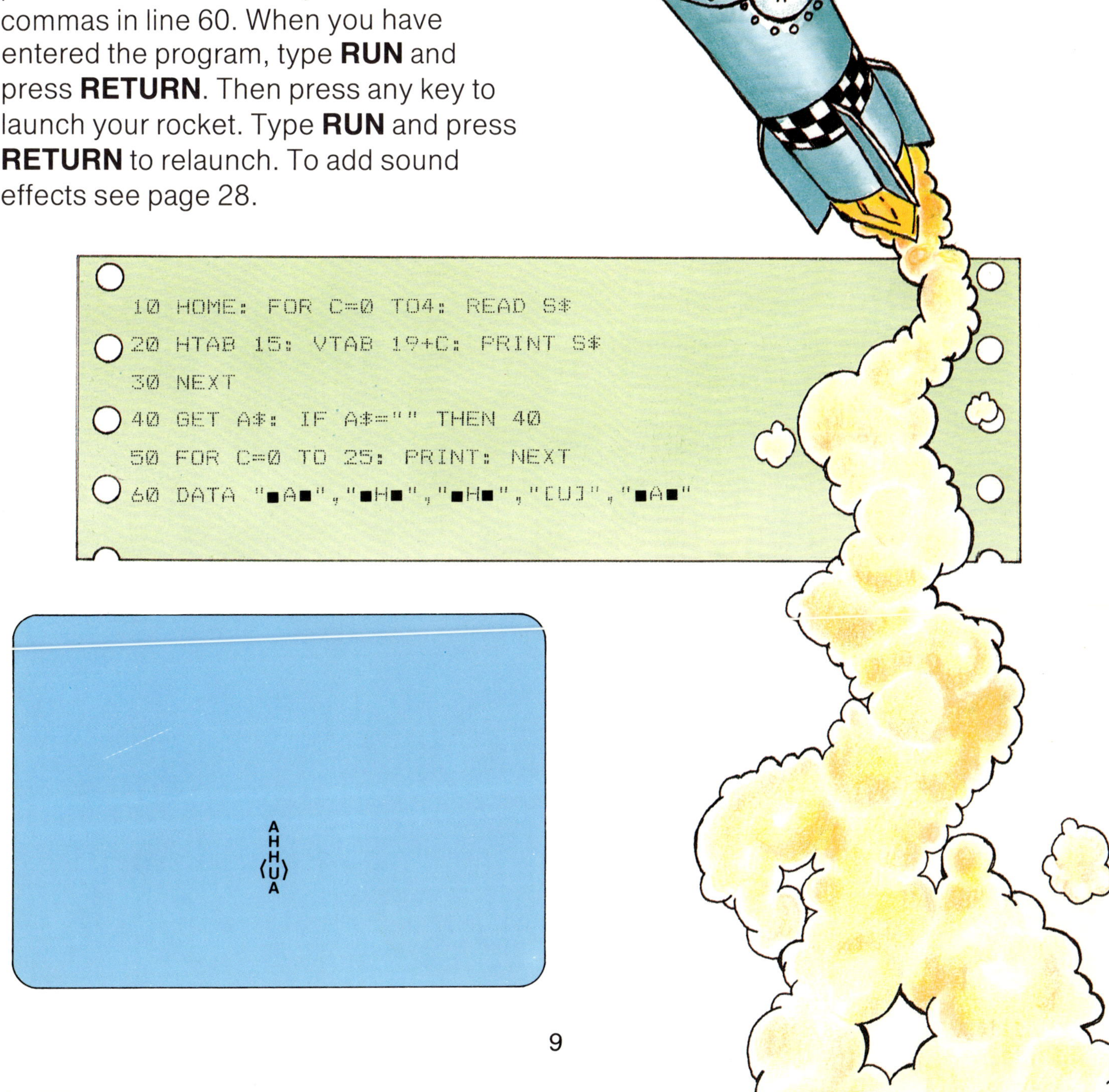

```
10 HOME: FOR C=0 TO4: READ S$
20 HTAB 15: VTAB 19+C: PRINT S$
30 NEXT
40 GET A$: IF A$="" THEN 40
50 FOR C=0 TO 25: PRINT: NEXT
60 DATA "■A■","■H■","■H■","[U]","■A■"
```

DOODLE-ART

Computers don't get bored but they're very good at doodling. All you have to do is watch. Is it a spaceship? A globe?

How it works

Enter the program, type **RUN** and press **RETURN**. A question mark will appear at the bottom of the list. Type in any number and press **RETURN**. Then let the computer start doodling. When it finally stops, press **CONTROL** and **RESET** together then type **RUN** and press **RETURN** and the computer will do you another doodle! Turn to page 29 for extra program lines which will give you different doodles.

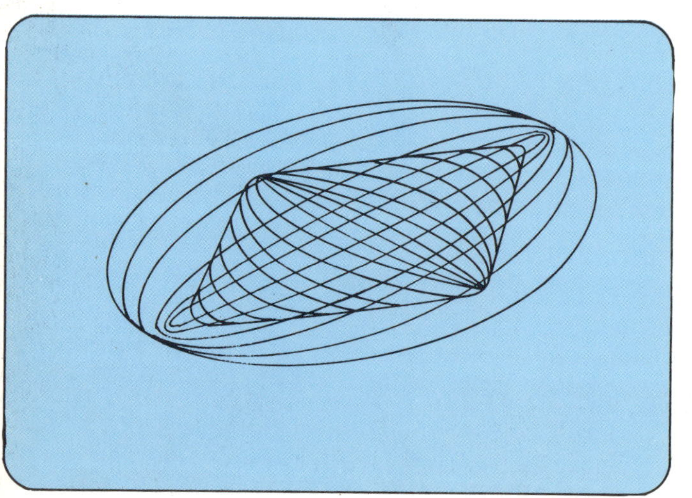

10 INPUT A: B=A/1.05: R=1
20 HGR: HCOLOR=3: HPLOT 140,159
30 FOR T=0 TO 3000 STEP .1
40 R=R*.999
50 X=SIN(T/A)*139*R+140
60 Y=COS(T/B)*79*R+80
70 HPLOT TO X,Y: NEXT

JUNGLE FLORA

Even a short program can give spectacular results. This is computer flower power at its most brilliant! Watch your screen gradually fill up with fantastic flowers, large and small, which appear in all the colors of the rainbow.

Enter the program, type **RUN** and press **RETURN**. The computer will keep making flower circles until you press the **CONTROL** and **RESET** keys together to stop it. To get a different fantastic result, turn to page 29. Add the 3 extra lines to this program and another jungle will grow before your eyes.

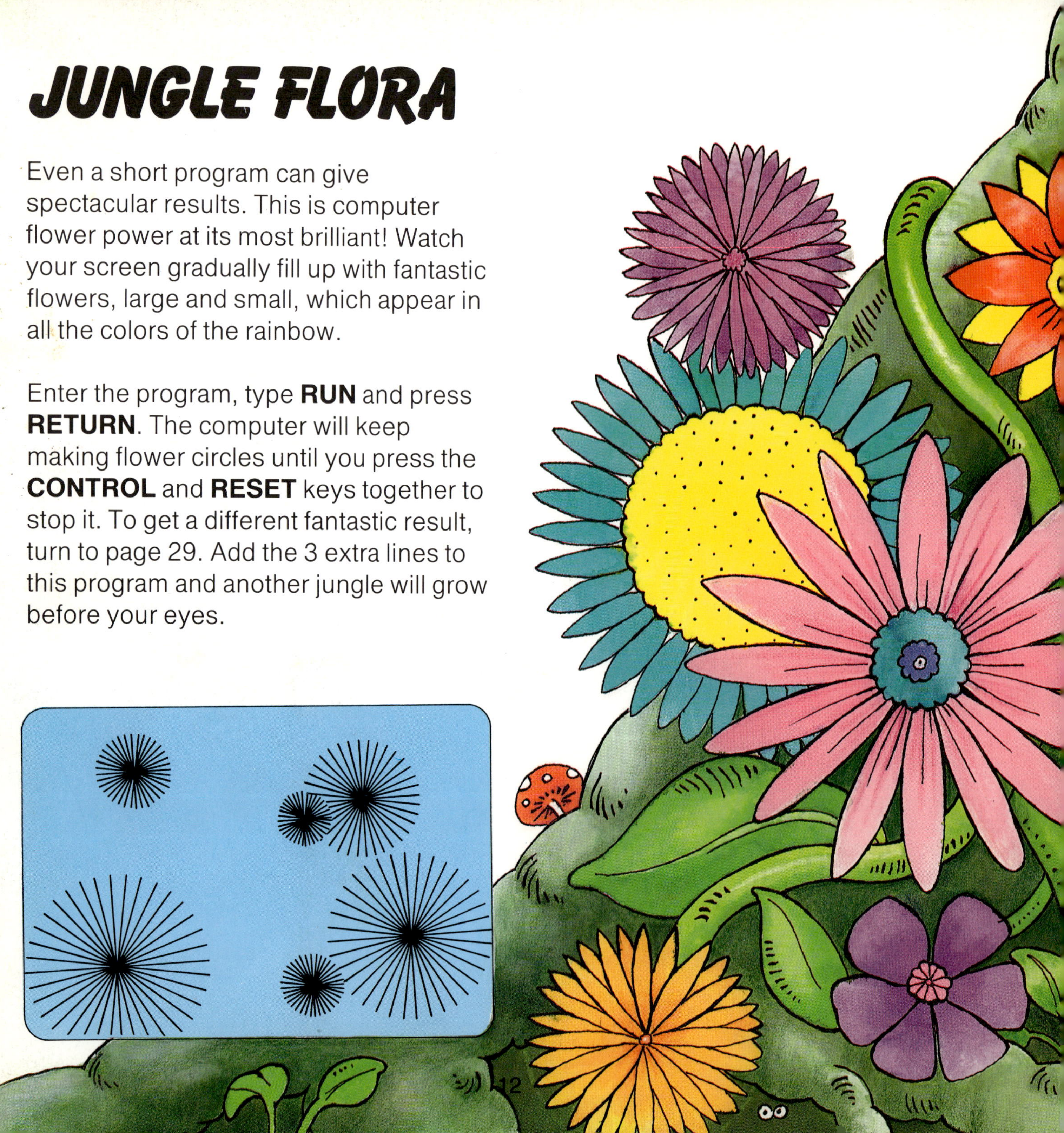

10 PI=3.1416: HGR2
20 R=RND(1)*70+5: X=RND(1)*280
30 Y=RND(1)*191:   C=RND(1)*8: HCOLOR=C
40 IF R+X>279 OR X-R<0 THEN 20
50 IF R+Y>191 OR Y-R<0 THEN 20
60 FOR A=0 TO 2*PI STEP PI/R
70 XC= R*COS(A): YC= R*SIN(A)
80 HPLOT X,Y: HPLOT TO X+XC,Y+YC
90 NEXT: GOTO 20

Look out for lines 40 and 50. They
look alike, but are not the same.

BUILDING BLOCKS

This builder seems to have made a mistake. See if you can do better. You can build anything by pushing the blocks around the screen.

How it works

Enter the program, type **RUN** and press **RETURN**. A block will appear on the screen. Move it using the **arrow keys** and press the **space bar** each time you need a new block. Press **CONTROL** and **RESET** together, then type **RUN** and press **RETURN** to start a new picture. See page 29 to add sound.

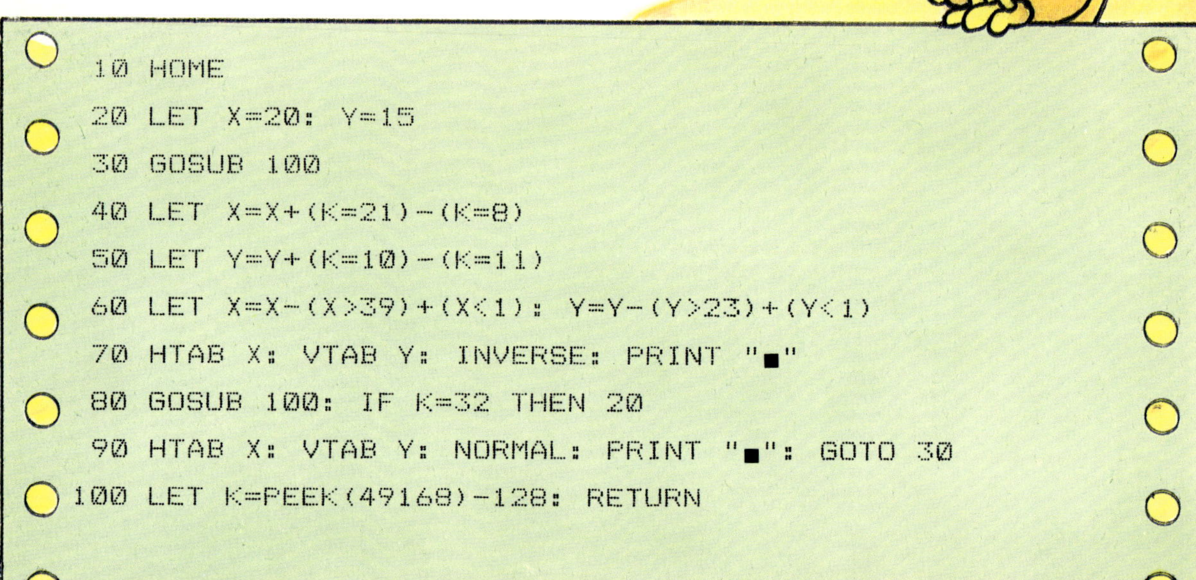

```
10  HOME
20  LET X=20:  Y=15
30  GOSUB 100
40  LET X=X+(K=21)-(K=8)
50  LET Y=Y+(K=10)-(K=11)
60  LET X=X-(X>39)+(X<1):  Y=Y-(Y>23)+(Y<1)
70  HTAB X:  VTAB Y:  INVERSE:  PRINT "■"
80  GOSUB 100:  IF K=32 THEN 20
90  HTAB X:  VTAB Y:  NORMAL:  PRINT "■":  GOTO 30
100 LET K=PEEK(49168)-128:  RETURN
```

THE PLAN

SHAPE-UP

Draftsman Dave is in a mess. It has taken him hours to draw all his polygons and now they're ruined. He needs a computer to help him out.

How it works

Enter the program carefully, then type **RUN** and press **RETURN**. Choose a number for the sides of the polygon and type it in. Pick a new number to start another shape.

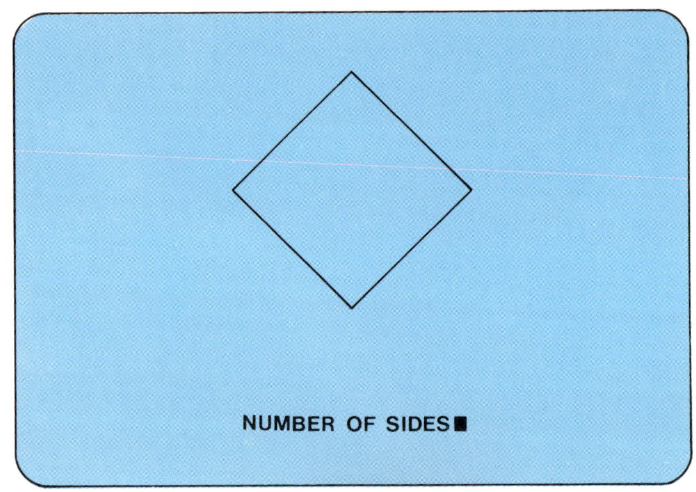

```
10 P=6.28
20 VTAB 24: HTAB 6
30 INPUT "NUMBER OF SIDES ";S
35 HOME: HGR: HCOLOR=7: HPLOT 128,1
36 FOR R=69 TO 70
40 FOR T=0 TO P+.01 STEP P/S
50 HPLOT TO SIN(T)*R+128,COS(T)*-R+71
60 NEXT T,R: GOTO 20
```

SKETCH PAD

Try this program as an alternative to crayons, felt tips and pencils. Get your model posed and hit the keys!

How it works

Enter the program, type **RUN** and press **RETURN**. Use the **arrow keys** to draw with. Hold them down for a continuous line. For diagonal lines use a **vertical** and **horizontal arrow key** alternately. To change the color of the line, press the **space bar** and choose a number between **0** and **7**. Colors **0** and **4** are black and can be used to erase lines. To start again press **CONTROL** and **RESET** together, type **RUN** and press **RETURN**.

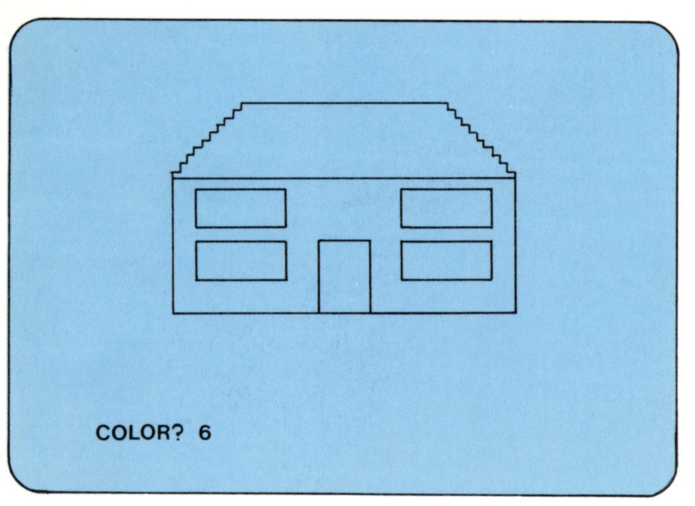

10 HGR: HOME: X=129: Y=96: C=3
20 HPLOT X,Y: HPLOTX+1,Y: HPLOT X,Y+1
30 HPLOT X+1,Y+1: GET K$: K=ASC(K$)
40 HCOLOR=C
50 X=X-2*((K=8 AND X>0)-(K=21 AND X<255))
60 Y=Y-2*((K=11 AND Y>0)-(K=10 AND Y<159))
70 IF K<>32 THEN 20
80 HTAB 5: VTAB 24: INPUT "COLOR ";C: GOTO 20

BLACK HOLE

Beware the black hole diving deep down through space. Watch the screen as the program runs and you might start to feel as if you are falling through space – on and on through endless darkness . . . . If you look carefully you will see how the optical illusion is created.

```
 10 FOR A=768 TO 777
 20 READ M: POKE A,M: NEXT
 30 POKE 232,0: POKE 233,3
 40 HGR2: HCOLOR=3: ROT=0
 50 FOR S=5 TO 22: GOSUB 90: NEXT
 60 FOR S=6 TO 22: GOSUB 90
 70 FOR D=1 TO (22-S)*20: NEXT
 80 GOSUB 90: NEXT: GOTO 60
 90 SCALE=4*S: XDRAW 1 AT 140,96: RETURN
100 DATA 1,0,4,0,58,36,45,54,7,0
```

How it works

Enter the program, type **RUN** then press
RETURN. A tunnel of squares will appear
on the screen. One after the other, from
smallest to largest, the squares will
switch off, then start over again.

FLYING DUCK

Your computer duck won't wreak havoc like this one. Watch it flap its wings realistically as it flies from one side of your screen to the other.

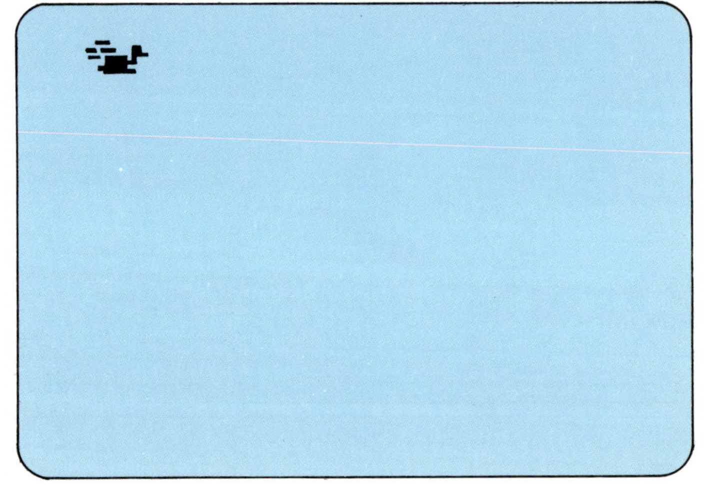

How it works

Enter the program, taking extra care with the numbers in lines **50** to **70**. Type **RUN** and press **RETURN** to make your bird fly across the screen. Press the **CONTROL** and **RESET** keys together, then type **RUN** and press **RETURN** to start it again.

```
10 FOR A=768 TO 812: READ M: POKE A,M
20 NEXT: POKE 232,0: POKE 233,3: HGR
30 HCOLOR=3: SCALE=2: FOR X=0 TO 270 STEP 6
40 LET S=1: GOSUB 80: S=2: GOSUB 80: NEXT: END
50 DATA 2,0,6,0,25,0,45,21,63,223,119,173,53,37,44
60 DATA 54,37,44,50,5,32,44,46,5,0,109,73,9,173,63
70 DATA 223,219,119,45,45,45,30,63,63,14,45,30,63,7,0
80 GOSUB 90: FOR D=1 TO 200: NEXT: GOSUB 90: RETURN
90 XDRAW S AT X+4*(S=1),50: RETURN
```

BEANSTALK

Jack's magic beanstalk had nothing on the ones you can create on your screen! New leaves sprout and grow before your very eyes with astonishing speed.

How it works

Enter the program, type **RUN** and press **RETURN**. A shoot will pop out from the ground and start to grow. To start again press **CONTROL** and **RESET** together then type **RUN** and press **RETURN**. A different beanstalk appears every time.

10 HGR: HCOLOR=1: POKE 49234,0
20 FOR Y=191 TO 170 STEP -1
30 HPLOT 0,Y TO 279,Y: NEXT
40 LET X=INT(RND(1)*200)+40
50 FOR Y=170 TO 20 STEP -1
60 X=X+INT(RND(1)*3)-1
70 HPLOT TO X,Y TO X+1,Y
80 IF RND(1)<.08 THEN GOSUB 120
90 NEXT: HCOLOR=2: FOR A=0 TO 6.3 STEP .2
100 HPLOT X,Y TO X+15*SIN(A),Y+15*COS(A)
110 NEXT: END
120 D=X+30: IF RND(1)<.5 THEN D=X-30
130 HPLOT TO D,Y-5: FOR L=0 TO 6.3 STEP .1
140 LET B=3*COS(L)
150 LET A=(3+RND(1)*9)*SIN(L)
160 HPLOT D,Y-5 TO A+D,Y+B-5
170 NEXT: RETURN

IS IT ART?

Arthur the artist is mucking up his masterpiece. Who needs canvas? Who needs paint? Create your own modern art without the splashes – just use your computer and this program.

How it works

Enter the program and then type **RUN** and press **RETURN**. Move the little dot with the **arrow keys** to the position you want and hit the **space bar**. Type in the number of sides, the diameter (**30-100**) and the color (**0-7**). Colors **0** and **4** are black. Move the dot to start a new shape. Be careful not to start any big shapes near the edges.

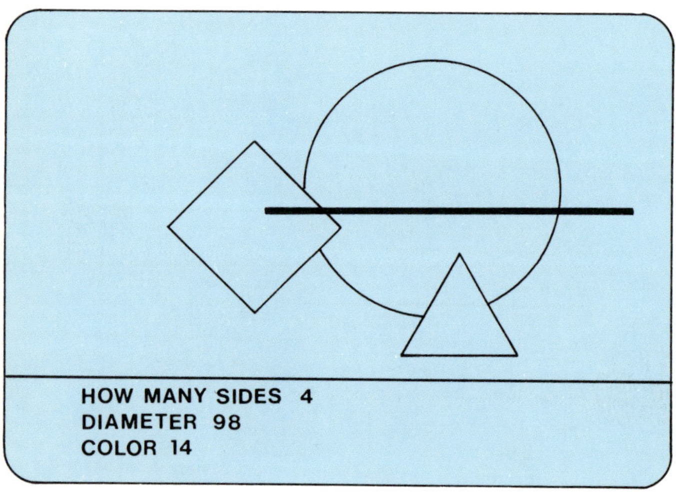

10 HGR: HOME: X=128: Y=96: P=6.28
20 HPLOT X,Y: GET K$: K=ASC(K$)
30 HCOLOR=0: HPLOT X,Y: HCOLOR=3
40 X=X-2*((K=8 AND X>0)-(K=21 AND X<255))
50 Y=Y-2*((K=11 AND Y>0)-(K=10 AND Y<159))
60 IF K<>32 THEN 20
70 HTAB 5: VTAB 24: INPUT "NO OF SIDES■";S
80 HTAB 5: INPUT "DIAMETER■";D
90 HTAB 5: INPUT "COLOR■";C
100 HCOLOR=C
110 HPLOT X,Y: FOR R=0 TO D/2
120 FOR T=0 TO P+.01 STEP P/S
130 HPLOT TO SIN(T)*R+X,COS(T)*-R+Y
140 NEXT T,R: HOME: GOTO 20

EXTRA BITS FOR ADDED FUN

These are additions to some of the programs which give extra effects. Number the lines exactly as they are shown here. The extra lines for Rocket and Building Blocks add sound effects. The additions for the Doodle-Art program will change the kind of doodle it makes. If you want to see a jungle with more unusual shapes, then add the extra three lines for Jungle Flora and see what the computer comes up with.

You don't have to type out the whole program again to fit in the additions. Just list the program and type the extra lines at the end. The computer will automatically put them into the right place.

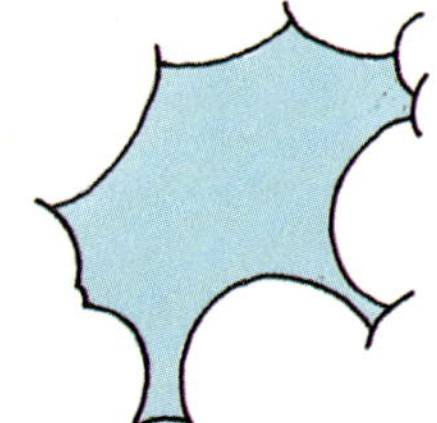

ROCKET

Page 9

```
45 PRINT CHR$(7): FOR D=0 TO 999: NEXT
50 FOR C=0 TO 25: PRINT
55 FOR S=1 TO 10: X=PEEK(-16336): NEXT S,C
```

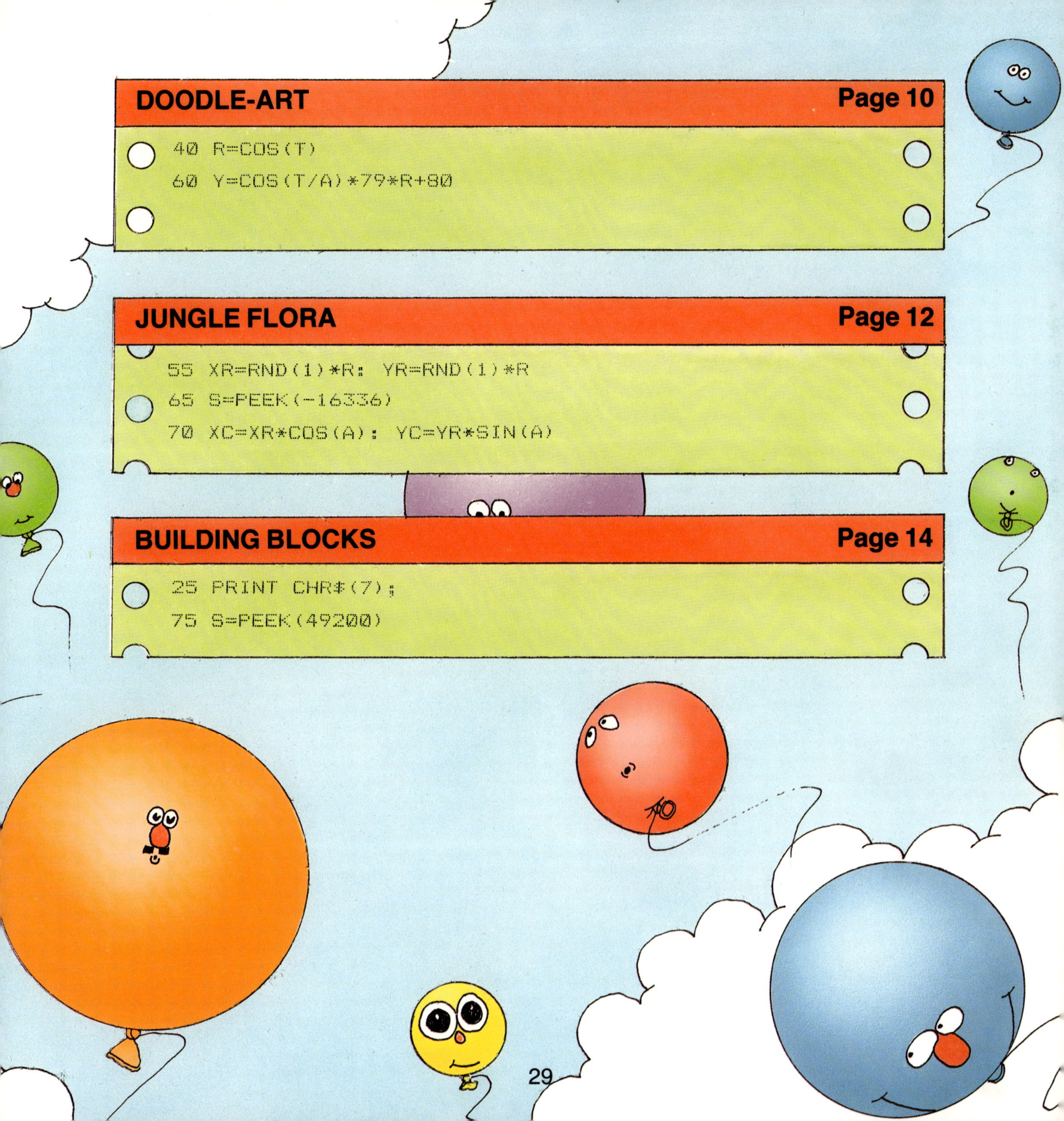

DOODLE-ART   Page 10

40 R=COS(T)
60 Y=COS(T/A)*79*R+80

JUNGLE FLORA   Page 12

55 XR=RND(1)*R: YR=RND(1)*R
65 S=PEEK(-16336)
70 XC=XR*COS(A): YC=YR*SIN(A)

BUILDING BLOCKS   Page 14

25 PRINT CHR$(7);
75 S=PEEK(49200)

GLOSSARY

BUG A mistake. A bug in a program means that it won't work. When you check a program for bugs you have to make sure that you haven't typed in the wrong symbols somewhere.

CHARACTERS All the letters of the alphabet, punctuation marks, numbers and signs which you can type in.

CURSOR This is the small square symbol on the screen which shows where the characters you type in are going to appear.

ESCAPE You must press this key before pressing the up **arrow key** if you are correcting a program on the screen.

HOME When you type HOME the screen is cleared and the cursor goes back to the top left-hand corner.

LINE Each line in a program starts with a number. A program line can be very long, taking up several lines of writing on the screen. A program line is finished when you press **RETURN**.

LIST You type in the instruction LIST when you want to see the program written out on the screen.

LOAD When you want to use a program that has been recorded on tape you have to LOAD it into the computer. When you type LOAD you are telling the computer to LOAD the program into its memory.

NEW When you type in NEW you are telling the computer to throw away the program in its memory to make way for a new one.

PRINT This instruction tells the computer to print words and numbers on the screen (not on paper.) Anything inside quotes will be printed exactly as you type it.

PROGRAM A set of instructions that the computer remembers.

RESET You can press this key, together with **CONTROL**, to clear the screen and reset the computer.

RETURN You press the **RETURN** key at the end of every program line. It tells the computer that the line is completed.

RUN When you type in RUN you are telling the computer to carry out the instructions you have given it in a program.

SAVE If you don't want to type a program all over again you can SAVE it by recording it onto tape.

INDEX